# RED PANDA

## ANIMALS KNOWLEDGE SERIES

### By

### DEUTSCHE DON JUAN

# Red Pandas

Aside from the giant black and white pandas, there also is the red panda, which is a small, solitary creature slightly larger than a domestic cat. This animal is closely related to raccoons, weasels and skunks, and is also distantly related to the more popularly known black and white panda. Its scientific name is Ailurus fulgens which literally means "shining cat." The red panda is most active during the wee hours of the night, i.e., from dusk to dawn. Hence, it is mostly sedentary during the day. The red panda is an animal considered endangered or threatened, and is believed to be one of the most vulnerable species.

# What Red Pandas Look Like

The red panda has soft reddish brown fur on the upper parts of its body. It also has blackish fur on its lower parts. Its head and body have a combined length of around 20 to 26 inches, with a long, shaggy and bushy tail that measures around 12 to 20 inches. It has a light face that is similar to a raccoon's; its face also has tear markings, as well as robust cranial-dental features. The red panda also has an extended wrist bone that works almost similar to a thumb; this wrist bone helps the red panda get a better grip.

# What They Eat

Red pandas mainly eat fresh chutes and bamboo leaves (which makes up 95% of their diet), and can also feed on birds, flowers, berries, eggs, and small mammals. Red Pandas are also unable to digest cellulose, similar to the giant pandas, so they should eat a lot of bamboo to survive. They digest bamboo shoots better than leaves. Their diets are supplemented by insects and fish. Red pandas have low-calorie diets so what they eat and sleep most of the time. They also find it important to be within close proximity of water; they usually drink once a day at the very least.

# Where Red Pandas Live

Red pandas have large ranges for areas wherein to live; they usually dwell in the cool temperate Himalayas forests, and reside on the foothills of western Nepal and Bhutan. Their area also extends to China, specifically on Yunnan, Sichuan, and Xizang provinces in the east. The slopes of these mountains trap water from monsoons, and bamboo understories grow in these forests to provide most of the red panda's diet. Hence, red pandas tend to stay within these areas due to their dependence on the growth of the bamboo shoots. They live together with giant pandas in their secluded, rainy, high-altitude forests.

# Social Life and Interaction

Red pandas interact a lot with other organisms. Red pandas are the predators of small animals such as birds and insects. On the other hand, they serve as prey for bigger cats such as clouded leopards and snow leopards. Owls and hawks also see them as prey. Red pandas are not seen as a prey by a lot of other animals because they stay mostly high up in the trees and are therefore beyond the reach of larger predators. Red pandas are mostly solitary unless it's mating season. During mating season, they are usually found in small groups.

# Mating Season for Red Pandas

The red pandas' mating season starts in January and ends in March. During the courtship period, the female will leave a heavy scent to mark her territory. The male will afterwards make a mark over her mark by urinating or by rubbing themselves over those areas. Red pandas will interact more every day before the mating process, and the courtship will last for several hours. The development period can range from 112 days to 158 days. During that period, the mother panda will appear tired and heavy. Births mostly take place in the summer and spring seasons; most of the newborn red pandas will be born in June.

# Red Panda Babies

Mother pandas usually give birth to 2-4 cubs. At birth, the baby red pandas usually weigh around 4 to 5 ounces. They are usually born blind and their eyesight develops only slowly. They are first covered with gray-buff fur, and will develop red hair after a few weeks. After 17 to 18 days, the eyes and the ears of the cubs will open. After 70 days, the cubs will have the full coloration of an adult red panda. Young red pandas remain in their nests for a period of 90 days and make their first excursion from their nest at night.

# Red Pandas' Behavior

The activities of red pandas change throughout the year depending on feeding regimes, temperature, and presence of offspring. Usually, red pandas are solitary, and are more active during the night as well as in the early hours of the morning. Red pandas tend to climb down trees headfirst; their flexibility is put to use as they jump from one branch to another. Red pandas' tails are used for balance when climbing trees, and tails are seen as straight and horizontal when on the ground. Red pandas are most active after eating and sleeping. They lick their whole body, wash their faces with their paws, and stretch their bodies against trees and rocks.

# Habitat of Red Pandas

Red Pandas live in forests around the Himalayas and mostly prefer temperate climates. They reside frequently in coniferous and deciduous forests and they tend to stay in an understory of hollow bamboo trees. Their habitat's average temperature is within 10 to 25 degrees Celsius, and the usual average annual rainfall is around 350 centimeters. Red pandas live in the same areas as giant pandas, but there is no competition between the two of them. To illustrate it better, both species of panda eat bamboo, but the giant pandas eat the upper portion of the plant and the red pandas eat the lower portion.

# Threats Faced by the Red Panda

The red panda has several predators, namely Asian golden cats, dholes (wild dogs), leopards and golden eagles. To add to the list, the yellow-throated marten is also known to kill and eat newborn red pandas. The climate change also affects their chances of survival; unusual weather patterns, global warming, and forest fires are common factors. Red panda numbers may have dwindled by as much as 40% within the last 50 years due to loss of habitat. Red pandas tend to climb trees, or strike out with their claws. Unfortunately for red pandas, they also get caught in traps originally meant for deer and wild pigs and they end up getting killed in the process.

# The Senses of a Red Panda

The red panda may be an excellent tree climber, but it actually has poor eyesight, and its senses of hearing and smell are not fully-developed. When the red panda senses danger, it tries to escape by climbing trees and hiding in tree hollows. In cases wherein it is no longer able to hide, it will just stand on its hind legs so that it will appear larger than it really is. It will also use its razor-sharp claws on its front paws to defend itself from any danger. The claws can actually inflict major injury on anything who tries to make a meal out of a red panda.

## Red Panda Health Conditions

Red pandas don't grow as fast as other animals do. They would only reach adult size after a year. Like people, red pandas also encounter health issues. They face high infant mortality. Young red pandas may experience lack of vitality because of maternal neglect or lack of lactation. Sometimes they may also have shallow bite wounds whenever their mother tries to carry them. However, if the mother gets too stressed, she may tend to overgroom the young cubs and this has resulted in them losing their ears or tails. The first few days of a red panda's life are the most critical; 19% are stillborn or die almost immediately after they are born.

# The Lifespan of a Red Panda

Red pandas are usually born during the early summer months. They usually weigh 110-130 grams at birth, and may grow 7-20 grams a day. Red pandas will also be independent after 8 months, and will reach their sexual maturity when they reach 18-20 months. The average lifespan of a red panda, when in the wild, is around 8 to 10 years, but it can reach a maximum lifespan of 14 years. If in captivity, the red panda may live for up to 13.4 years. Records show that the oldest red panda was in the Netherlands; he lived up to 21 years and 7 months while staying at the Rotterdam Zoo.

# A Red Panda's Evolution

Red pandas are said to be distantly related to the giant pandas. They appear to have evolved in the areas of Western Europe and Pakistan. Fossils similar to that of the red panda have been found in Eastern Europe and in the western part of North America. It's hard to determine where to classify the red panda; there have been debates whether they are closer to the raccoon family or to the bear family. However, more recently, it has been decided through careful research that the red pandas are more closely related to animals such as otters, weasels, skunks and raccoons.

# Red Panda Precautionary Measures

Yes, the red pandas may be cute, but they actually pose more danger than you think they could. People should minimize physical contact with red pandas; physical contact with humans may stress the red pandas out and may lead to them being aggressive. Red pandas must be regarded with caution because they have extremely strong jaws and sharp claws that can injure people. They could also become highly aggressive especially if they sense a need to defend themselves or their young. There have been recorded attacks on humans by red pandas in captivity.

## Red Panda Diseases

Red pandas also face certain diseases, especially when they reach the adult stage. Having diseases may be the most harmful instance during normal situations. They may experience having health problems such as fatty livers, gastric ulcers, heart diseases, and hair loss (mainly on their tails). If infants will not receive enough colostrum, they will be infected. They may also experience respiratory diseases such as pneumonia, osteoarthritis, and dental diseases/periodontitis. Some of those diseases are infectious ailments such as the Canine Distemper virus. Red pandas can also be threatened by parasitic diseases such as heartworm, lungworm, and ringworm. Those diseases have resulted in high mortality rates among red pandas.

# Hunting Red Pandas

Red pandas are considered vulnerable. Their numbers are slowly dwindling due to different factors. Illegal hunting is one of the main threats to red pandas. They are sometimes killed for their coats which are used for making fur clothing. They are also hunted by some for the illegal pet trade, as well as for their bushy tail which is highly valued (The tail is used for making hats which are considered good luck charms for Chinese newlyweds.). Also in China, red panda fur is used for cultural ceremonies. In a wedding, and the bridegroom usually wears the hide of a red panda.

# The Red Panda Reproduction Process

When a female red panda reaches 18 months of age, she is by then ready to reproduce. She will be fully matured when she reaches 2 to 3 years of age. Red pandas only interact with one another during the mating season. Otherwise, they are solitary animals. Females become lethargic usually around 6 weeks before giving birth. A few days before a female gives birth, she will start collecting materials such as grass, brushwood, and leaves to build her nest. The young cubs will stay with their mother until it's time for her to give birth once again. Males don't really help out with raising their young; they would only do so if they are in pairs or in small groups.

## What Scientists Say about Red Pandas

The red panda has given scientists and researchers a great taxonomic debate. They all initially thought that the red panda is a close relative of the giant panda, but according to recent studies, genetics has shown that red pandas are more closely related to weasels and raccoons. Like these animals, red pandas have ringed tails. The red pandas are a part of their own unique family which is the Ailuridae. Fossil evidence pertaining to red pandas is scarce, but findings suggest its relation to Procyonidae (raccoons). Some molecular studies support relationships to other small animals such as Mustelidae (weasels) and Mephitidae (skunks).

# Fun Facts about the Red Panda

Here are some fun facts you probably didn't know about the red panda.

☐ Have you seen the animated movie "Kung Fu Panda?" Do you remember Master Shifu (voiced by veteran actor Dustin Hoffman)? Shifu is actually a red panda but most people don't know that.

☐ Red pandas are also known by the following names: Bright Panda, Bear-cat, Cat-bear, firefox, Lesser Panda, Poonya, and Petit Panda.

☐ A red panda is about the size of a raccoon.

☐ Baby pandas are usually born inside trees.

☐ Most of their time is spent in trees; they can sleep inside trees, and can curl up like cats so they will stay warm.

# Comprehension Questions

1. When does the mating season for red pandas start? -- In January

2. How old was the oldest red panda? -- 21 years and 7 months

3. What do you call a young / baby red panda? -- Cub

4. When will the cubs have the full coloration of an adult red panda? -- After 70 days

5. When is a red panda ready to reproduce? After 18 months of age

6. What does the scientific name of the Red Panda mean? -- Shining cat

7. What color is the fur on the red panda's upper parts of the body? -- Reddish-brown

8. What is the typical maximum lifespan of a red panda? -- 14 years

9. On which month are the newborn cubs usually born? -- June

10.     Aside from fresh chutes, what do red pandas usually eat? -- Bamboo

Made in the USA
Lexington, KY
11 April 2016